abandoned angel

Also by Burt Kimmelman

POETRY

Musaics (1992)

First Life (2000)

The Pond at Cape May Point (2002)

Somehow (2005)

There Are Words (2007)

As If Free (2009)

The Way We Live (2011)

Gradually the World: New and Selected Poems, 1982–2013 (2013)

CRITICISM

The Poetics of Authorship in the Later Middle Ages: The Emergence of the Modern Literary Persona (1996)

The "Winter Mind": William Bronk and American Letters (1998)

The Facts on File Companion to 20th-Century American Poetry (2005, Editor)

The Facts on File Companion to American Poetry (2007, Co-Editor)

The Encyclopedia of American Poetry (2013, Co-Editor)

William Bronk in the Twenty-First Century: New Assessments (2013, Co-Editor)

The Poetry and Poetics of Michael Heller: A Nomad Memory (2015, Co-Editor)

Machaut's Legacy: The Judgment Poetry Tradition in Late Medieval Literature (2016, Co-Editor)

abandoned angel

NEW POEMS

Burt Kimmelman

MARSH HAWK PRESS

East Rockaway, New York • 2016

Marsh Hawk Press books are published by Poetry Mailing List, Inc., a not-for-profit corporation under section 501(c)3 United States Internal Revenue Code.

Cover artwork: *Strange as Angels,* by Jane Kimmelman; copyright © Jane Kimmelman 2016
Cover and book design: Susan Quasha; copyright © Susan Quasha 2016

Art photography: Dennis Donahue; copyright © Dennis Donahue 2016

Library of Congress Cataloging-in-Publication Data

Names: Kimmelman, Burt, author.
Title: Abandoned angel : new poems / Burt Kimmelman.
Description: East Rockaway: Marsh Hawk Press, 2016.
Identifiers: LCCN 2016019420 | ISBN 9780996427531 (pbk.)
Classification: LCC PS3561.I4233 A6 2016 | DDC 811/.54—dc23 LC record available at https://lccn.loc.gov/2016019420

7 6 5 4 3 2 1 FIRST EDITION

Marsh Hawk Press
P.O. Box 206
East Rockaway, New York 11518-0206
www.marshhawkpress.org

Acknowledgments

Gratitude to the publishers and editors of these journals in which some of these poems have appeared, at times in earlier versions:

Boog City, Golden Handcuffs Review, Home Planet News Online, House Organ, Local Knowledge, Marsh Hawk Review, Noon, Verse-Virtual: An Online Journal of Poetry.

Special thanks to Thomas Fink and Sherry Kearns for their guidance when reading this book in various stages of its development.

Cover and book design by Susan Quasha
Cover artwork, *Strange as Angels,* by Jane Kimmelman
Art photography by Dennis Donahue

Publication of this book was supported in part by a generous grant from the Community of Literary Magazines and presses via the New York State Council on the Arts.

For Diane and Jane, as always

Tot torn meillui et esmori

In Memoriam

Thomas Elias Weatherly, Jr.
1942–2014

:the tension of fucking
springs to.

Contents

Weather

Cities

abandoned angel

Weather

Snow Squall

Swirl of birds
swerves apart
in white air.

February, New Jersey

Trees lean over the road,
twigs and branches holding
the sunlight in our days

of white taut cold, the snow,
the afternoon not so
bare, the night not so close.

Notre-Dame du Haut, Ronchamp

Le Corbusier Show, *Centre Pompidou*, 7.24.15

> *One and*
> *one, two,*
> *three.*
>
> —ROBERT CREELEY

Sun on stone
and windows—

light strikes through
until dark—

looking out,
looking in.

Topanga Canyon, Mid July

Sun in the doorway, shrubs and trees,
cactus reaching up, red flower
on top, distant mountain beyond,
puffs of white cloud, blue sky, cool air—

we sit looking out, sip our tea,
wait for the humming bird who will
hover in the low branches, its
long bill drawing the day's nectar.

Sandy's *Bashö in America*

After reading Sander Zulauf's haikus

Modest and true words,
they are more than the poet—
wet stone in moonlight.

From Shore

Miami Beach

Small green waves
lapse on shore—
beyond them

heads, shoulders
rise and fall—
a gull glides

above, just
for now, some
long white clouds.

Photos from Somewhere

A friend I have not
seen in forty years
sends me some photos
of himself, others
I knew, I know—their

faces suddenly
come to life before
I can tell who they
are—someone who
might be me, grown old.

The Early Spring

The snow has gone—
the sun shines each

day between rains—
bare twigs reach up.

Man and Woman Reclining

After a pen-and-ink drawing in one of
Fay Jones's notebooks

In our sleep we fold ourselves over
our dreams—to hold them, protect them. At
times I see you in my dream. Do you
see me too? They are there as we lie
over them—and we are there, dreaming
the same dream. No one else dreams our dream.

They are there and we are there too. Our
eyes are closed, and if we opened them
they would be gone. Would you be gone too?

Dawn

Once asleep
the dream becomes
the first birds' chirps
in the darkness

and then the thoughts
of the day past
and what must be
done—suddenly

there is the dawn
light behind leaves
on branches, dark
becoming green.

In the Night

In the night I
watch myself sleep.
Awake, I see
me in my dream

and I think my
dream is enough.
At times I yearn
to live in dreams—

to live in their
mute enchantment.
Although we cry
out in our sleep

sometimes, we feel
we belong there.
We live as one,
sleepless, sleeping.

Winter Solstice

At dawn branches
and fog are there,

the world once more,
land and sky one.

—New Jersey 2015

Abandoned Angel

Left behind in
the flurry of
parting, she slumps
over the cold

stone—her heavy
wings, strange clothing,
the pink dawn more
strange in a world

The Start of Spring

Even now your lips remember
when they were blossoms.
And I remember when I would say
"Your lips are blossoms"

—MARK WEISS

The snow has left
us with the mud—
and in it we
find our cautious

joy, that the cold
is gone, the light
is here to stay,
and the first peeps

before dawn I
hear, opening
the door to look
out, are signals

of a new world
soon in flower—
lush ground waiting
for the warm sun.

Utanasana

standing
sitting
walking
& lying down

—Paul Blackburn

Folded over,
I see the hands
of an old man
grasping his feet,

and hear his breath
not yet quite stilled,
even, not what
I remember—

hard to believe
so much time has
passed, hard now not
to remember

what I once was,
and death so much
less than what it
was, this morning.

February Morning

Snow-tinged bamboo
leaves hold the gray
sky even when
the breeze stirs them.

I Fold Myself Around You

I fold myself around you
the way the nights fold themselves
around the days. Just when we

think we will not go on much
longer we do. The moment
of life is long. People live

on. We think of them. I think
of you and you are there. You
live on. I, too, somehow, do.

Avocados, Winter

Leather orbs
green and brown
in lamplight

cast across
the kitchen
table this

winter night—
we await
spring's shy warmth.

Late October, Northern New Jersey

Gray day, trees
far off sway
in a breeze—

their red leaves,
above them
bare branches—

before long
traceries
in white sky.

Bear Mountain, Early November

Cobble of milky way.

—GARY SNYDER

Climb by stones, tree
roots in fallen

leaves—sun comes through
branches above.

The Great Blue Heron

After erasures in a letter from Madeline Tiger

I often see
when walking my
dog not only
geese and mallards

Great Blue Heron
in a distance
such that one might
not even notice

him standing there
neck so high stretched—
yesterday I
saw another

in the water
stepping along
dipping for fish
then up as fast.

Quarrel of Gulls

Miami Beach, January

Sky blue where green ocean
reaches, a white sail just
barely moves, some swimmers
rise and fall past the waves,
the rest of us lying
on sand in sun. We are

here, the gulls gone after
screeching over a bit
of food, lifting apart
from each other, wings out
in a sudden swirl,
then flying off as one.

Late Morning

Susan Bee's *Garden of Delights*

Sky and road—
sun, clouds, trees—
we hold hands.

"The Luxury of Time"

"European Clocks and Watches"
at the Met, December 2015

How innocent they were,
learning complexity,
not merely beautiful
gears turning together—
one another as one—
but our intricacy.

Why imitate the sun
when earth's white ceramic
pastures lay there before
them—idyls with satyrs
at rest—or a flower
exquisitely jeweled.

Petals opened to our
gaze—a kind of music,
the wings of Keats's bird
flutters in the autumn
dusk all in a moment—
a dream's measure in gold.

Morning in Maplewood, Early Summer

Already light when I awake,
I sit below our maple tree
drinking my tea. The air is cool
for the season and I am glad

to hear the birds' various chirps
and whirls. A high pitched banter—same
note, same note—stabs at the day, and
a whistling loops across the yard.

Train to Tours, July

Sun through white clouds
along the sky,
yellow wheat fields,
green tufts of trees

all in a row,
red tiled roofs,
chimneys—concrete
water towers

and idle farm
equipment here
and there—beyond
the tracts of land

a distant road,
some small cars glide
by on their way
back toward Paris.

Early November, Light

Maplewood, New Jersey

Red leaves
the start

of light
squirrels

tumble
over

the limbs
of trees

leap to
wires

along
the street—

how not
to be

still.

Train Home from the River

Tigre, outside Buenos Aires,
late afternoon

Sun still hot through
the windows—he
slumps over his
backpack, eyes closed.

Arrival of a Transport, Thereisenstadt Ghetto
by Leo Haas, 1942-1944

> Reading the New York Times during a blizzard, 2016

1.

Delicate lines
tell us in black
ink what there is
to know—barren

trees, bared branches
bending over
a road winding
through white wash, far

past fields of snow
the horizon
vague, possibly
where the journey

into winter's
darkness on foot,
in the cold, has
long been begun.

2.

In the foreground
a single light
before a house
covered in snow

at the road's end
might make shadows
through a tree just
beyond at dusk—

and up the road
in the trees bent
people marching,
led by soldiers,

one with rifle,
motorcycle
ahead of him,
but mostly trees.

3.

A dark parade
of inked captives
behind the trees
along a road

meandering
through countryside
until scant strokes
of the pen cease

where the eye falls—
toward a dark sky
figures of some
birds appear, take

shape in distance,
in a somber
light—ink and wash
merged, nothingness.

4.

I lie in bed
as I read my
newspaper—snow
falling outside,

past my window
in silence, white
for the moment,
for the morning—

casual lines,
these playful lines,

the intricate
trees what I see.

I should not look
more closely but
I do, knowing.
I am helpless.

February, Train to Ghent

Strand of empty
trees in a green
field, muddy ditch
near—passing my

window—they are
there and I am
here, the warm car
rocking gently,

the muffled pitch
of wheels on steel
tracks, civilized
travelers reading

their books or phones,
out of the rain,
a gray day like
the day before.

Commute

I head home, think
of you there, what we

will say—that we
eat the night's stars.

The World at Dawn

I wanted so ably
to reassure you

[. . .]
                    and got
up, and went to the window,
pushed back, as you asked me to,

the curtain, to see
the outline of the trees
in the night outside.

—ROBERT CREELEY,
FROM "THE WORLD"

Lying still
on my bed,
I look through

my window.
Outside, trees
stand into

the sky, their
branches and
leaves above

roofs, chimneys.
The dawn is
white. I am

looking out
on the world.
There is its

light. A car
goes by not
far away.

I might say
something like,
if I were

dying, "I
will leave this
world." The word

world is so
important
for poets—

some knew it
was a word.
Stevens, Bronk

and Oppen,
Creeley are
all gone. They

thought about
words. They knew
how very

desperate
words are. Their
words are mine.

I lie still
and I say
that the world,

its light, is
out "there," and
I want it.

Cities

From Above, Looking North Up the Westside Highway, Evening Rush Hour

Whitney Museum, Mid December 2015

> *It's a strange courage*
> *you give me, ancient star....*
>
> —WILLIAM CARLOS WILLIAMS

Red lights in
rows, dark sky,
further north

white lights cross
the river—
it's a strange

courage I
am given,
in night's glow.

On a Subway Train to Brooklyn, Evening Rush Hour

He has wrapped his arm around her—
and she sinks into his shoulder.

We watch her face—when his fingers
trace her bare chest in light touches.

She lets him and their eyes close—while
he thinks of her breasts, their softness.

They spread their legs—waiting for home
on a Monday night, to eat, sleep.

Early Autumn

The rain tells us
"let go"—as it
runs to ground through
the city's grates.

July's late light
like memory
dissolves—and
I look for dark.

Parc Jacques Brel, Brussels

End of January

Young men and women
have caught the metro
to their gentle jobs
in offices, well
past dawn. The park is

barren in the gray
light, too early for
the children who run
and climb. I watch through
the Bar Beton's grand

window, sipping my
coffee. Some slow, smooth,
sweet jazz in between
conversation fills
the room, piano

and bass doing all
the work. Two women
in overcoats, head
scarves, stroll cobblestones
near the fence, their pace

keeping time (a new
birth of the cool, I

suppose). They talk as
they amble along,
whatever their cares.

On a Train Passing East Orange in Snow

White sky above
steeple and trees—

lace branches sway
in my window.

German Tourism 1940, Krakow

From a photograph at the Schindler Museum

Caught at their leisure
strolling through town, they
have spotted a Jew
venturing out. One
soldier has brought his

scissors. Passersby
are paused to watch. He
is standing still, arms
by his sides, looking
into winter gray

air in his black hat,
black coat—the young man
snipping the sidelocks
carefully gathered,
in his concentration

war, the world, briefly
gone. His friends smile
at the camera,
a forgotten hand
resting on a sleeve.

Jazz on a Tuesday Evening in South Orange

The Gregg Buford Quartet

Horn's sounds fill the room, drums,
voices I used to hear.

The dead stay dead but we
are so much more alive.

This is what music is.
We always want to live.

Manhattan Evening Just Before Christmas

Faces on Seventh Avenue
in the winter holiday lights,
children perfectly still before
Macy's window display, Thirty-

Fourth Street a racket of traffic
and jay-walkers, I glide below
ground at Penn Station, catching my
train back home to a quiet night.

Regatta on Lake Union, Late July

The light on the lake
dazzles us, who look
on from the shore, yet
the wind is what we
want, that comes and goes.

—Seattle, 2013

Taking Off from Orly Airport

Out and back the mind

—WILLIAM BRONK

The city below,
the houses among

the mists of morning,
the stands of trees and,

as we ascend, the
wheat fields beyond them

all, the eye seeing
farther—we are just

as much there as here,
alien and true.

Putting Down in Brussels, January

We get back from wandering
the walks in rain, and the shops
not far off—the chilly day
turned dark, we watch from four flights
above through a window, drops
of water falling past light
from the streetlamp just below.

Cleo at about 6:13

Un salut à Agnes Varda

She barely hears her voice
from the jukebox across
the room, the light outside
as bright as the music
and her summer white dress
and blonde coiffure She

holds a glass of brandy
she seems not to know is
there, her fingertips just
above the stem. She glides
past the people who talk
or read their newspapers

at the café's small round
tables and into a chair,
takes off her sunglasses
and swallows her drink, then
covers her eyes to step
out to the boulevard.

Piazza Verdi, Sun

Trieste, 18 April 2014

Empty coffee cups,
left over breadsticks—
pigeons snatch at crumbs
and someone strolls by—
hills and sea beyond.

Robert Gober Show in Late October

La douçor et la melodie
Me mist ou cuer grant reverdie.★

—GUILLAUME DE LORRIS

Sunlight on the tracks,
birds chirping their songs,
I wait for the train
to take me somewhere
else—at the MOMA

sinks and wallpaper,
playpens we stop, look
at, something all wrong
with them but so what?
It could have been spring,

the joyous flitting
of birds here and there,
as if somehow we
all want to be fooled—
the city, too, in light.

★"The sweetness and melody of the song [of spring's birds] filled my heart with [blissful music]" (from *The Romance of the Rose*, 13th century, trans. Douglas Kelly)

Subway to Bryant Park in May

I am among my people
—HARVEY SHAPIRO

Late spring and we all want
to be out. On the train
platform a couple swings

to steel drums. In the park
we stroll under the trees,
lie on the grass in sun.

First Warm Day in April on West Twenty-Third Street

Below the curlicued
facades of brick buildings—
rows of narrow windows—

a man stands in the sun,
smiling at a dollar
bill he holds with both hands.

Not Having Seen the On Karawa Show
at the Guggenheim, This 12th of February

I think not to mark this
day in the cold winter
although to write it down
as if I had lived it
is more than I should have
to do yet here I am.

Sunday in Liers, Early May

Some miles from Antwerp

They take their time
on a Sunday—
mid afternoon
in the *grote markt*.

How kind early
May weather can
be—the strolling
by, the sitting.

In a warm light
green, blue, red drinks
are served—each in
its special glass.

We will forget
for a moment—
everything—
nothing for it.

Musée d' Orsay, Fifth Floor*

April 2014

There are reflections
in sunlight through trees,
faint divinings—but
indoors no mirrors.
Young couples hold one

another, gazing
at green gardens framed
on the gallery
walls—the day's shapes. I
stroll past them, looking.

---

* Impressionist collection

Sunday Morning in Krakow

A train ride back
from Auschwitz last
evening where we
stood within walls—

we listened how
the weakest slept
on the bottom
tier in the mud

yet the top tier
was really no
better in cold
Polish winter

under a roof
that let in snow.
Just then heavy
rain held us up—

kept us to wait
in a darkness.
Of course there were
horrors I will

not name—too late.
Morning's bells are
full of grief I
take with my tea.

About the Author

PHOTO: DIANE SIMMONS

BURT KIMMELMAN was born and raised in New York City after the Second World War. His eighth collection of poetry *is Gradually the World: New and Selected Poems, 1983–2013* (BlazeVOX, 2013). His poems have been featured on National Public Radio and are often anthologized. A number of interviews of him are available in print or online.

He teaches literary and cultural studies at New Jersey Institute of Technology, and in all has published seventeen books of poetry and criticism as well as more than a hundred articles on literature and other matters. He lives in Maplewood, New Jersey with his wife, the writer Diane Simmons. More about him can be found at BurtKimmelman.com.

TITLES FROM MARSH HAWK PRESS

Jane Augustine, *KRAZY: Visual Poems and Performance Scripts, A Woman's Guide to Mountain Climbing, Night Lights, Arbor Vitae*

Tom Beckett, ~~DIPSTICK~~ *(DIPTYCH)*

Sigman Byrd, *Under the Wanderer's Star*

Patricia Carlin, *Quantum Jitters, Original Green, Second Nature*

Claudia Carlson, *Pocket Park, The Elephant House*

Meredith Cole, *Miniatures*

Jon Curley, *Hybrid Moments*

Neil de la Flor, *An Elephant's Memory of Blizzards, Almost Dorothy*

Chard deNiord, *Sharp Golden Thorn*

Sharon Dolin, *Serious Pink*

Steve Fellner, *The Weary World Rejoices, Blind Date with Cavafy*

Thomas Fink, *Selected Poems & Poetic Series, Joyride, Peace Conference, Clarity and Other Poems, After Taxes, Gossip: A Book of Poems*

Norman Finkelstein, *Inside the Ghost Factory, Passing Over*

Edward Foster, *Sewing the Wind, Dire Straits, The Beginning of Sorrows, What He Ought To Know, Mahrem: Things Men Should Do for Men*

Paolo Javier, *The Feeling Is Actual*

Burt Kimmelman, *Somehow, Abandoned Angel*

Burt Kimmelman and Fred Caruso, *The Pond at Cape May Point*

Basil King, *The Spoken Word/the Painted Hand from Learning to Draw/A History 77 Beasts: Basil King's Bestiary, Mirage*

Martha King, *Imperfect Fit*

Phillip Lopate, *At the End of the Day: Selected Poems and An Introductory Essay*

Mary Mackey, *Travelers With No Ticket Home, Sugar Zone, Breaking the Fever*

Jason McCall, *Dear Hero,*

Sandy McIntosh, *A Hole In the Ocean: A Hamptons' Apprenticeship, Cemetery Chess: Selected and New Poems, Ernesta, in the Style of the Flamenco, Forty-Nine Guaranteed Ways to Escape Death, The After-Death History of My Mother, Between Earth and Sky*

Stephen Paul Miller, *Any Lie You Tell Will Be the Truth, There's Only One God and You're Not It, Fort Dad, The Bee Flies in May, Skinny Eighth Avenue*

Daniel Morris, *If Not for the Courage, Bryce Passage, Hit Play*

Sharon Olinka, *The Good City*

Christina Olivares, *No Map of the Earth Includes Stars*

Justin Petropoulos, *Eminent Domain*

Paul Pines, *Divine Madness, Last Call at the Tin Palace, Charlotte Songs*

Jacquelyn Pope, *Watermark*

George Quasha, *Things Done For Themselves*

Karin Randolph, *Either She Was*

Rochelle Ratner, *Ben Casey Days, Balancing Acts, House and Home*

Michael Rerick, *In Ways Impossible to Fold*

Corrine Robins, *Facing It: New and Selected Poems, Today's Menu, One Thousand Years*

Eileen R. Tabios, *The Connoisseur of Alleys, Sun Stigmata, The Thorn Rosary: Selected Prose Poems and New (1998–2010), The Light Sang As It Left Your Eyes: Our Autobiography, I Take Thee, English, for My Beloved, Reproductions of the Empty Flagpole*

Eileen R. Tabios and j/j hastain, *the relational elations of ORPHANED ALGEBRA*

Susan Terris, *Ghost of Yesterday, Natural Defenses*

Madeline Tiger, *Birds of Sorrow and Joy*

Tana Jean Welch, *Latest Volcano*

Harriet Zinnes, *New and Selected Poems, Weather Is Whether, Light Light or the Curvature of the Earth, Whither Nonstopping, Drawing on the Wall*

YEAR	AUTHOR	MHP POETRY PRIZE TITLE	JUDGE
2004	Jacquelyn Pope	*Watermark*	Marie Ponsot
2005	Sigman Byrd	*Under the Wanderer's Star*	Gerald Stern
2006	Steve Fellner	*Blind Date With Cavafy*	Denise Duhamel
2007	Karin Randolph	*Either She Was*	David Shapiro
2008	Michael Rerick	*In Ways Impossible to Fold*	Thylias Moss
2009	Neil de la Flor	*Almost Dorothy*	Forrest Gander
2010	Justin Petropoulos	*Eminent Domain*	Anne Waldman
2011	Meredith Cole	*Miniatures*	Alicia Ostriker
2012	Jason McCall	*Dear Hero,*	Cornelius Eady
2013	Tom Beckett	~~DIPSTICK~~ *(DIPTYCH)*	Charles Bernstein
2014	Christina Olivares	*No Map of the Earth Includes Stars*	Brenda Hillman
2015	Tana Jean Welch	*Latest Volcano*	Stephanie Strickland

ARTISTIC ADVISORY BOARD

Toi Derricotte, Denise Duhamel, Marilyn Hacker, Allan Kornblum *(in memorium)*, Maria Mazzioti Gillan, Alicia Ostriker, Marie Ponsot, David Shapiro, Nathaniel Tarn, Anne Waldman, and John Yau.

For more information, please go to: **www.marshhawkpress.org**